Heartland Quilts

Rescued Treasures from the Midwest

by Lila Lee Jones

CHITRA PUBLICATIONS

Your Best Value in Quilting

www.QuiltTownUSA.com

D1473544

Chitra Publications
2 Public Avenue
Montrose, Pennsylvania 18801-1220

First Printing 2003

Library of Congress Cataloging-in-Publication Data
Jones, Lila Lee.
    Heartland quilts : rescued treasures from the Midwest / by Lila Lee
Jones and the editors of Traditional Quiltworks.
       p. cm.
    ISBN 1-885588-47-X (pbk.)
    1. Patchwork—Patterns. 2. Quilting—Patterns. 3. Quilts—Middle
West—History—19th century. I. Traditional quiltworks. II. Title
TT835 .J652002
746.46'09788—dc21
                    2002013364

Edited by: Debra Feece & Virginia Jones
Design and Illustrations: Brenda Pytlik
Photography: Van Zandbergen Photography, Brackney, Pennsylvania
and Guy Cali Associates, Inc., Clarks Summit, Pennsylvania

Our Mission Statement:
We publish quality quilting magazines and books
that recognize, promote, and inspire self-expression.
We are dedicated to serving our customers
with respect, kindness, and efficiency.
www.QuiltTownUSA.com

Introduction

For many years I longed for antique quilts but rarely found one I could afford. The few that were within my price range were in deplorable condition. When the really good ones were put on the auction block, the prices soared. Fortunately, I attended so many auctions throughout the years that I occasionally found affordable 19th-century quilt tops and stacks of blocks that had been stored away, some of them none too ceremoniously. These I rescued by quilting them lovingly and compiling what I knew about their stories. I then added them to my quilt collection.

There are purists who would not "destroy" the integrity of a 19th-century quilt top by quilting it. But I feel that quilt tops and assembled groups of blocks should be quilted, used carefully, and enjoyed as they were meant to be—as quilts.

There is nothing more rewarding than to find a top or a set of blocks that begs to be quilted. In my opinion, the feel of soft vintage cotton fabric and the delight of the needle flying quickly through the layers cannot be matched by a new quilt. Even with reproduction fabrics, I feel something is missing. Perhaps it is the bond that is created between the present-day quilter and the person who pieced the blocks many years earlier. My only regret is that I do not know the names of those wonderful women who moved to the American Heartland and pieced the treasures I love today.

Because each of my quilts has a story to tell, I cannot share their beauty and simplicity without sharing their stories—where and in what condition I found them and what I had to do to rescue them. Rarely in perfect condition, most needed lots of TLC. Although there are quilts that are lovelier and quilted to perfection, my rescued treasures are now ready to hand down for posterity. It is my dream that these quilts and the versions you make of them will inspire a new generation of enthusiastic quilters.

Lila Lee Jones

Patterns

True Lover's Knot 4

Missouri Daisy 6

Ocean Waves 8

Lucky Lindy 10

Road to California 12

Dove in the Window 14

Dresden Plate 16

Tulips 18

Ariel's Blankie 20

Neckties 22

Rocky Road to Kansas 24

General Directions 31

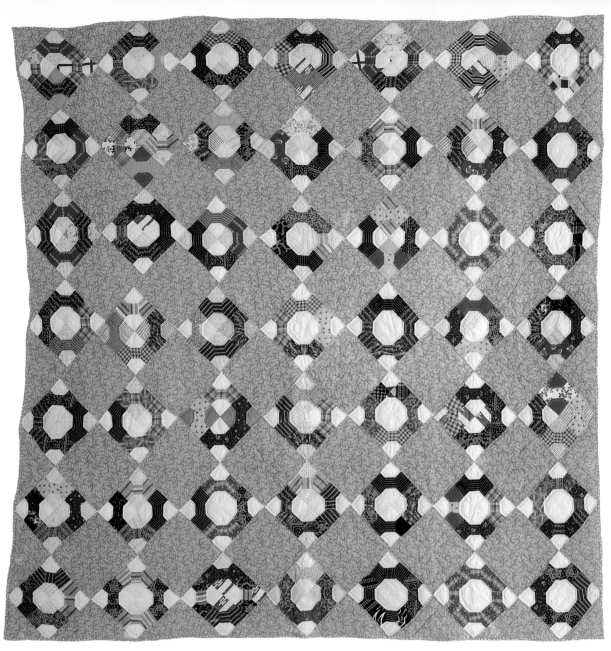

"True Lover's Knot"

On a warm spring day, I waited until an auction in Butler, Missouri, was almost over to buy this 1890s quilt top. The auctioneers kept passing it by to sell other things, but I waited patiently. At last I had to ask them to sell it when I noticed they left it hanging on the porch railing and began to move toward the backyard to sell the furniture. Another quilter had spotted the "True Lover's Knot" quilt top and wanted it, too, but when the auctioneer cried "sold!" I took it home for $35.

I recognized fabrics from as early as the 1870s. Unfortunately, a mouse had chewed a hole in one of the blocks. Luckily I was able to mend it with fabric from a circa 1878 apron which matched it perfectly. Washing the top removed minor stains as well as its old, musty smell. Then I laid it in the sunlight on a sheet, wrong side up, to dry before I began quilting.

The needle woman who pieced the top so many years ago set the blocks in what is known as The True Lover's Knot, which has a Snowball inside each block. Her stitches were excellent—much better than I could have done—and her

choice and placement of colors were outstanding. Her "humility block" is quite obvious. In one corner of the quilt, she deliberately made one mistake in setting her Bow Tie blocks together. To emphasize it further, she placed the deep, golden yellow which shouts "Look at me!" in that corner of the quilt.

The alternate squares are made from fabric that has a delicate fern design. When I first thought of quilting the top, I debated about adding a border in order to use the quilt on my three-quarter sized bed. However, the longer I debated about the border, the more I knew the quilt had to stand on its own as that long-ago quilter had pieced it. I considered using the 1878 apron for the binding, but the fabric was too thin and didn't look good when I tried it around the edge of the quilt. Instead, I used a piece of fabric that wasn't quite as old. It seemed just right because it had the same shade of delicate color found in the fern pattern fabric.

This quilt is one of the good old oldies in my collection of antique quilts, and the mellow reds and dark blues are nearly as bright today as they were when it was first pieced.

4

True Lover's Knot

This quilt would make a perfect wedding gift.

QUILT SIZE: 69 1/4" square
BLOCK SIZE: 7" square

MATERIALS

- Assorted dark prints totaling at least 2 1/2 yards
- Assorted light prints and solids in white, tan, and yellow, totaling at least 2 yards
- 2 1/2 yards first pink print
- 3/4 yard second pink print for the binding
- 4 1/2 yards backing fabric
- 73" square of batting

CUTTING

The hand-piecing patterns (on page 26) are full size and do not include a seam allowance. Make a template for each pattern piece. Trace around the template on the wrong side of the fabric and add a 1/4" seam allowance when cutting the fabric pieces out. All other dimensions include a 1/4" seam allowance.

For each of 196 Bow Tie Units:
- Cut 2: A, dark print
- Cut 1: B, same dark print; or cut a 1 5/8" square
- Cut 2: A, light solid or print

Also:
- Cut 36: 7 1/2" squares, first pink print
- Cut 2: 5 7/8" squares, first pink print, then cut them in half diagonally to yield 4 corner triangles
- Cut 6: 11 1/4" squares, first pink print, then cut them in quarters diagonally to yield 24 setting triangles
- Cut 8: 2 1/2" x 44" strips, second pink print, for the binding

DIRECTIONS

For each Bow Tie Unit:
- Stitch a dark print B between 2 matching dark print A's.

- Set in 2 light print or solid A's to complete a Bow Tie Unit, as shown. Make 196.

- Lay out 4 Bow Tie Units so they form a ring. Stitch them into pairs and join the pairs to complete a True Lover's Knot block. Make 49.

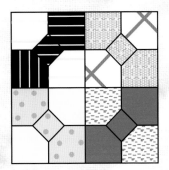

ASSEMBLY

- Lay out the blocks on point in 7 rows of 7. Place the 7 1/2" pink print squares between the blocks. Place the setting triangles along the edges and the corner triangles in the corners.
- Stitch the blocks and triangles into diagonal rows and join the rows.
- Finish the quilt as described in the *General Directions*, using the 2 1/2" x 44" second pink print strips for the binding.

Assembly Diagram

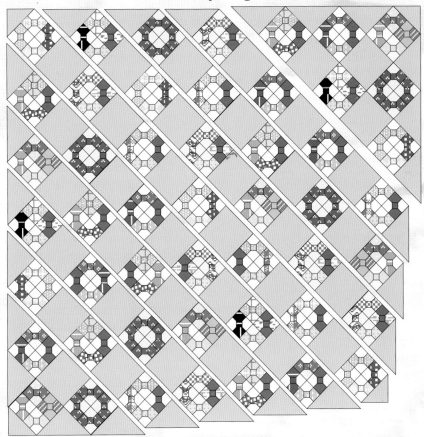

5

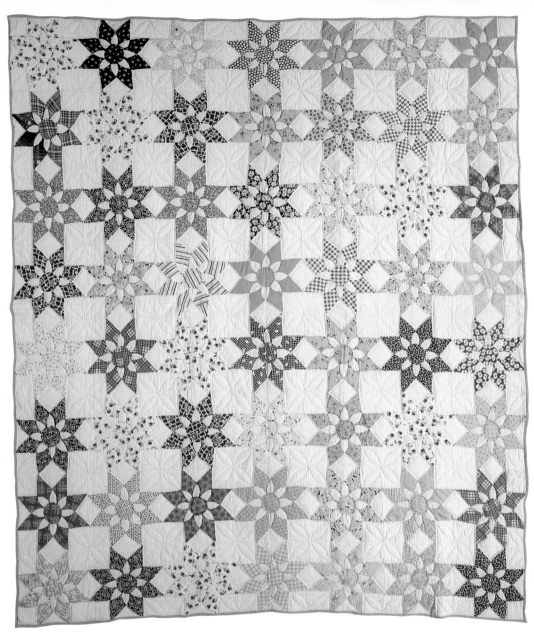

"Missouri Daisy"

"Would you be interested in buying a quilt top?" a friend asked on the phone one spring morning. I dropped everything and hopped into my car to drive out to her home in the country. When I arrived there, she told me that an aunt had died and she had to dispose of her household possessions. My friend didn't quilt and wanted to keep only the quilts her mother had made for her.

I was immediately intrigued by the muted colors of "Missouri Daisy," which blended so well together, they almost appeared to have been dipped in tea. The fabric was soft to the touch, and I knew at once that it was made entirely by hand with fine cotton from the late 1920s.

When I paid her for it, almost as an afterthought she produced a Blazing Star quilt top which her grandmother had made when she was over 80-years old. I bought it, too, though its bright colors made me cringe. By comparison, the muted tones in the Daisy were quiet and satisfying.

For a long while I debated about adding a border to "the Daisy," but each time I spread it out on the bed, I put it away. Something was not quite right. I quilted the Blazing Star during a dreary November, but the Daisy still waited for

me. The next summer I brought out the Daisy once again when it finally dawned on me that it needed to be washed. My friend's aunt had used the quilt top for a summer spread for many years and it was simply dirty.

Now washing an antique quilt top, even by hand, can be a tricky business, but I had made up my mind to do it. It's hard on the seams and puts stress on the tiny pieces. After seven rinsings, the water finally ran clear, and I carefully took the fragile quilt to the patio floor where I spread it atop a white sheet to dry. Its colors started singing out strong and clear, and the fine sugar sack fabrics were very white except for a few Pure Cane Sugar stamps with holly wreaths.

"Missouri Daisy" sprang to life as it had when the quilter made it over 70 years ago. I recognized fabrics from the twenties smiling up at me from the patio floor. It was then I knew the quilt wouldn't get a border and I would quilt it exactly as the original quilter had pieced it, entirely by hand.

My pleasure with the quilt had just begun. When I'm quilting the soft cotton fabrics in the Daisy, my needle simply glides through them. What a joy it was as my tiny needle, with a mind of its own, flew through the cotton which had been used but not abused!

Missouri Daisy

Gathered petals add texture to these scrappy flowers.

QUILT SIZE: 71 3/4" x 82"
BLOCK SIZE: 10 1/4" square

MATERIALS
- Assorted pastel prints totaling at least 4 1/2 yards
- 5 1/2 yards muslin
- 3/4 yard blue print for the binding
- 5 yards backing fabric
- 76" x 86" piece of batting

CUTTING
The hand-piecing patterns (here and on page 28) are full size and do not include a seam allowance. Make a template for each pattern piece. Trace around the templates on the wrong side of the fabric and add a 1/4" seam allowance when cutting the fabric pieces out. All other dimensions include a 1/4" seam allowance.
For each of 56 blocks:
- Cut 8: A, pastel print
- Cut 1: C, same pastel print
Also:
- Cut 448: B, muslin
- Cut 224: 3 1/2" squares, muslin
- Cut 56: 5 1/2" squares, muslin, then cut them in quarters diagonally to yield 224 triangles
- Cut 8: 2 1/2" x 44" strips, blue print, for the binding

DIRECTIONS
For each block:
- Stitch 2 print A's to a muslin B, as shown. NOTE: *The B will not lie flat.* Make 4.

- Set a muslin triangle into each unit.

- Stitch muslin B's between the units, as shown.

- Set 3 1/2" muslin squares into the corners.

- Baste 3/16" from the inner edge of the petals. Pull the thread to gather the petals until the center of the Star lies flat.

- Turn under the edges of the matching print circle and appliqué it to the center of the Star, covering the gathered edges of the petals, to complete a Missouri Daisy Block. Make 56.

ASSEMBLY
- Lay out the blocks in 8 rows of 7. Stitch the blocks into rows and join the rows.
- Finish the quilt as described in the *General Directions,* using the 2 1/2" x 44" blue print strips for the binding.

**Full-size pattern B
for Missouri Daisy.
(Patterns A and C
are on page 28.)**

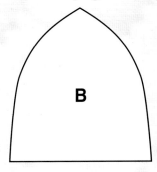

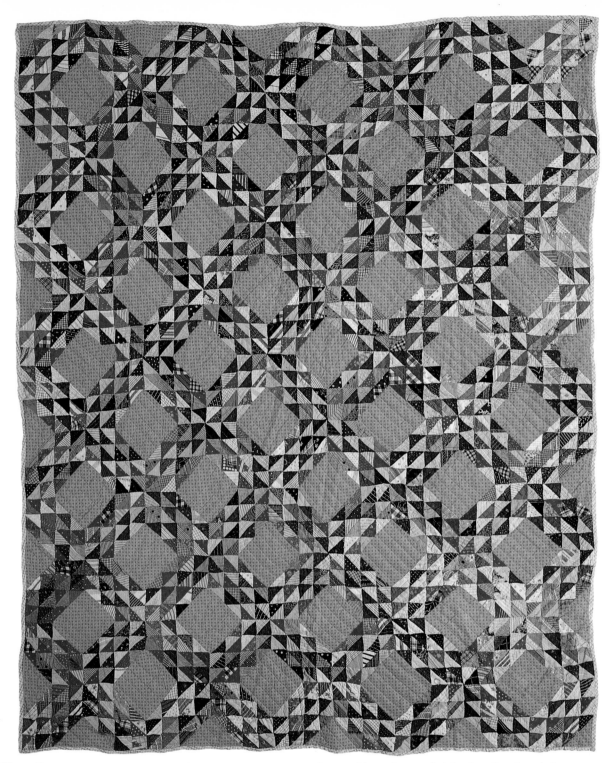

"Ocean Waves"

This is one of my favorite quilts and I loved it at first sight. It was completely finished and bound when I purchased it, which is unusual in my quilting life. It is done in all the traditional colors—bubble gum pink, many shades of blue, some blacks, and white—and all in tiny prints.

Upon seeing this quilt offered at an auction in a small Missouri town in Bates County near the Kansas border, I thought it surely would soar out of sight when the bidding began. But sometimes one becomes very lucky at small-town auctions. There were a number of other auctions in the area that day, and this one was not widely advertised.

When the bidding began, I held my breath. I had never been able to buy a finished quilt of such beauty at an auction, but some things are meant to be. Imagine my surprise when I purchased this hand-stitched Ocean Waves quilt for only $35!

It became one of my most important antique finds. This quilt will remain in my collection for as long as I maintain my home because it is truly representative of the work of women who lived in the Heartland during pioneer times. It represents the patience and precision of early-day quilters who kept every scrap of fabric to use in their quilts. I don't know the name of the quiltmaker, but her spirit lives on in this well-preserved quilt that was saved for "best." Today, I use it on an antique bed… for "best."

Ocean Waves

Bubblegum pink sets off this sea of scraps to perfection.

QUILT SIZE: 72" x 88"
BLOCK SIZE: 8" square

MATERIALS
- Assorted dark prints totaling at least 3 3/4 yards
- Assorted light prints totaling at least 3 3/4 yards
- 2 yards pink print
- 3/4 yard light plaid
- 5 1/2 yards backing fabric
- 76" x 92" piece of batting

CUTTING
Dimensions include a 1/4" seam allowance.
- Cut 124: 5 3/4" squares, assorted dark prints
- Cut 99: 2 7/8" squares, assorted dark prints, then cut them in half diagonally to yield 198 triangles
- Cut 124: 5 3/4" squares, assorted light prints
- Cut 99: 2 7/8" squares, assorted light prints, then cut them in half diagonally to yield 198 triangles
- Cut 40: 6 1/8" squares, pink print
- Cut 5: 9 1/4" squares, pink print, then cut them in quarters diagonally to yield 20 large triangles. You will use 18.
- Cut 1: 4 7/8" square, pink print, then cut it in half diagonally to yield 2 small triangles
- Cut 9: 2 1/2" x 44" strips, light plaid, for the binding

DIRECTIONS
- Draw diagonal lines from corner to corner on the wrong side of each 5 3/4" light print square. Draw horizontal and vertical lines through the centers.
- Place a marked square on a 5 3/4" dark print square, right sides together. Stitch 1/4" away from both sides of the diagonal lines, as shown. Make 124.

- Cut the squares on the drawn lines to yield 992 pieced squares. You will use 990. Press the seam allowances toward the dark prints.
- Lay out 4 pieced squares, as shown, and stitch them together to form a Unit A. Make 198.

- Stitch 2 Unit A's together, as shown, to complete a half-block. Make 49.

- Stitch 2 half-blocks together, as shown, to complete a Block A. Make 20.

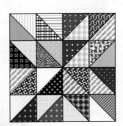

- Stitch 2 Unit A's together, as shown, to complete a half-block. Make 49. Set aside the 2 remaining Unit A's.

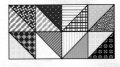

- Stitch 2 half-blocks together, as shown, to complete a Block B. Make 20.

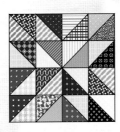

- Stitch a pieced square between 2 dark print triangles, as shown, to form a dark Unit C. Make 99.

- Stitch a pieced square between 2 light print triangles, as shown, to form a light Unit C. Make 99.

- Stitch dark Unit C's to opposite sides of a 6 1/8" pink print square.

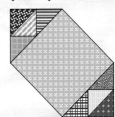

- Stitch light Unit C's to the remaining sides of the pink print square to complete a Block C. Make 40.

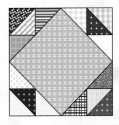

- Stitch a dark Unit C to the left side of a large pink print triangle, and a light Unit C to the right side of the large pink print triangle, as shown. Make 9.

(Continued on page 26)

9

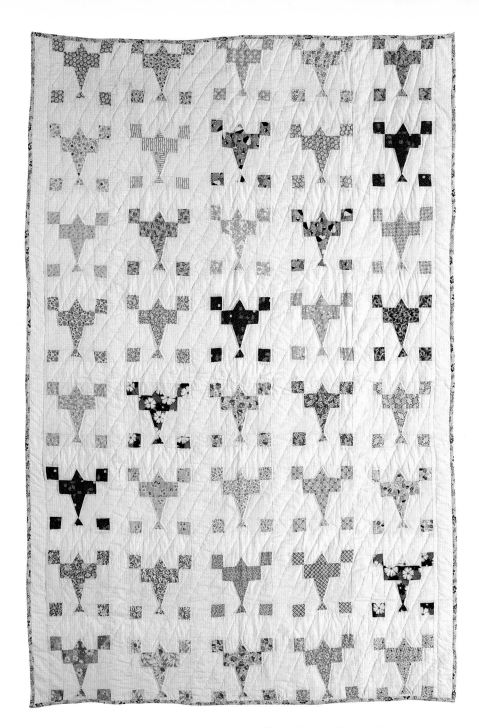

"Lucky Lindy"

The pattern for the Airplane block in "Lucky Lindy" appeared in The Kansas City Star newspaper shortly after Charles Lindbergh made his solo flight over the Atlantic in 1927. My husband purchased this quilt as a top at a farm sale in Kansas. With 40 small planes flying in formation, I felt it had to have been made for a boy's bed.

When I saw this fine work wasn't quilted, I became concerned that something might have happened to the quiltmaker. Perhaps a grandmother started making the quilt for a grandson long ago. She had put a white border around the planes, so I knew the design had been completed. But why didn't she quilt her top after she finished piecing it? Perhaps, she was one of the many who loved to piece quilts but didn't enjoy quilting on the large frames which took up so much room in small houses.

I made no effort to finish the quilt until my husband kept asking me about it. I added a layer of cotton batting, quilted the little planes, and used a blue and white print for the binding. Finally, "Lucky Lindy" was ready for our great-grandson's visit.

When he came to see us, I made him a place to sleep and spread the quilt over him. The uneven quilting designs, I explained to him, were clouds. He was delighted by the 40 little airplanes that march up and down the quilt like toy soldiers. Then I thought again about the original quiltmaker. Perhaps her grandson outgrew airplanes before she sat down to quilt her work. Whatever the reason, I'm glad she didn't finish her quilt because if she had, it would have perished long ago through hard use and constant laundering. Instead, it rests safely in my growing collection of quilts from America's Heartland.

10

Lucky Lindy

What young future pilot wouldn't love to curl up with this quilt?

QUILT SIZE: 51" x 75 3/4"
BLOCK SIZE: 7 1/2" square

MATERIALS
- Assorted prints, each at least 10" square
- 3 1/2 yards white
- 1/2 yard blue print for the binding
- 4 1/2 yards backing fabric
- 56" x 81" piece of batting

CUTTING

The hand-piecing patterns (on page 27) are full size and do not include a seam allowance. Make templates for each of the pattern pieces. Trace around the templates on the wrong side of the fabrics and add a 1/4" seam allowance when cutting the fabric pieces out. All other dimensions include a 1/4" seam allowance. Cut the lengthwise white strips before cutting smaller pieces from that fabric.

For each of 40 blocks:
- Cut 1 each: A, B, and C, one print
- Cut 1: 2" x 5" strip, same print
- Cut 4: 2" squares, same print

Also:
- Cut 6: 2 3/4" x 78" lengthwise strips, white
- Cut 40 each: D, DR, E, ER, F, G, and GR, white
- Cut 80: 2" x 5" strips, white
- Cut 35: 2 3/4" x 8" strips, white
- Cut 7: 2 1/2" x 44" strips, blue print, for the binding

DIRECTIONS
For each block:
- Stitch a print A between a white D and a white DR.

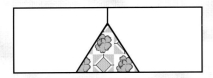

- Stitch the short seam between the D and DR.
- Stitch the 2" x 5" same print strip to the bottom of this unit.

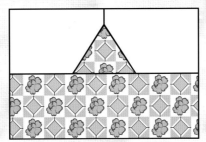

- Stitch the same print B between a white E and a white ER.

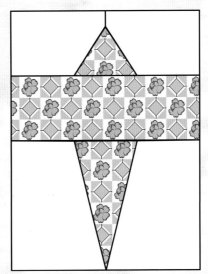

- Stitch this unit to the first unit, as shown.

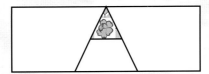

- Stitch the same print C to a white F, and then stitch the unit between a white G and a white GR.

- Stitch this unit to the bottom of the pieced section to complete a Plane Unit.

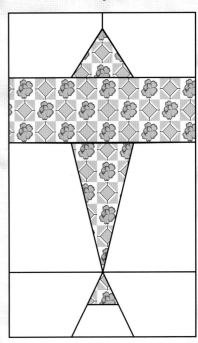

- Stitch 2" matching print squares to the ends of a 2" x 5" white strip. Make 2. Stitch them to the long sides of the Plane Unit to complete a Lucky Lindy block. Make 40.

ASSEMBLY
- Referring to the quilt photo, lay out 8 blocks in a vertical row with 2 3/4" x 8" white strips between them.
- Stitch the blocks and strips together to complete a vertical row. Make 5.
- Measure the length of the rows and trim the 2 3/4" x 78" white strips to that measurement. Lay out the vertical rows alternately with the white strips, beginning and ending with a white strip, and stitch them together.
- Finish the quilt as described in the *General Directions*, using the 2 1/2" x 44" blue print strips for the binding.

"Road to California"

Everyone liked this quilt top except me. For some reason I failed to find the colors pleasing. I think it was the dark shade of blue the quilter used for her alternate squares. At any rate, it came with a Pine Tree quilt top I really wanted. The quilt tops were among the last things to sell at an auction I attended north of Mound City, Kansas, late in the summer of 1996. I had decided that I would pay as high as $35 for the Pine Tree top but because I had waited patiently all day for the quilts to sell, I would have probably paid more for it if it had come to that.

When the auctioneers saw the quilt tops, the ring man rolled three of them into a wad and that is the way they sold. He didn't spread them out to show off their beauty and make the appropriate remarks. He didn't tell the buyers that they were made entirely by hand. Apparently, the auctioneers weren't particularly interested in anything except getting the last of the sale items disposed of as quickly as possible.

I bought all three of the very old quilt tops for a mere $12! When I went home, I spread them out on my bed and realized that the Pine Tree needed much more work than I had first thought. The Road to California quilt, however, needed nothing except quilting. So I worked on that one first.

Soon after I started, I became fascinated by the fabrics in the tiny Four Patches. The 19th-century red fabrics are alike, but the dark sections have different blues and blacks. They are solid with tiny, white patterns typical of the fabrics women used in dressmaking in those days. I soon realized that I had a truly unique antique quilt in my frame. The tiny flowers, dots, and geometric patterns in the blue and black prints were fun to quilt. The soft cotton fabric in the quilt top was typical of materials of that day and made my work easy.

Questions flooded my mind while I quilted, finishing what some quiltmaker had begun long ago. Was the quilt made for a child or perhaps a hired man's bed? Why wasn't it finished? I loved the way the quilter had put the quilt together so the white squares formed a trail across the top. I quilted them so that was accentuated. It was a joy to watch the quilt come to life. What began as a simple quilt made with Four Patch blocks has become a favorite of everyone who sees it.

Road to California

Chains of diagonal squares create energy in this simple-to-piece quilt.

QUILT SIZE: 69" x 81"
BLOCK SIZE: 4" square

MATERIALS
- 24 assorted navy prints, each at least 1 1/2" x 44" and totaling at least 1 1/8 yards. Use some black prints if desired.
- 2 1/2 yards navy print for the border
- 2 1/2 yards white
- 2 1/2 yards blue
- 2 1/3 yards red print
- 3/4 yard red for the binding
- 5 yards backing fabric
- 73" x 85" piece of batting

CUTTING
Dimensions include a 1/4" seam allowance. Cut the lengthwise navy, white, and red print strips before cutting smaller pieces from those fabrics.
- Cut 24: 1 1/2" x 44" strips, assorted navy prints
- Cut 4: 1 1/2" x 80" lengthwise strips, white
- Cut 24: 1 1/2" x 44" strips, white
- Cut 4: 1 1/2" x 80" lengthwise strips, navy print, for the border
- Cut 4: 1" x 80" lengthwise strips, red print
- Cut 304: 2 1/2" squares, red print
- Cut 152: 4 1/2" squares, blue
- Cut 8: 2 1/2" x 44" strips, red, for the binding

DIRECTIONS
- Stitch a 1 1/2" x 44" navy print strip to a 1 1/2" x 44" white strip along their length, to make a pieced panel. Make 24. Press the seam allowances toward the navy prints.
- Cut twenty-six 1 1/2" sections from each pieced panel for a total of 624. You will use 608.

- Stitch 2 sections together to form a Four Patch Unit. Make 304.

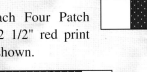

- Stitch each Four Patch Unit to a 2 1/2" red print square, as shown.

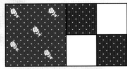

- Stitch 2 units together to complete a Road to California Block. Make 152.

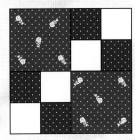

ASSEMBLY
- Lay out 8 blocks alternately with eight 4 1/2" blue squares, as shown, making sure the white squares are all oriented the same. Stitch them together to complete a row. Make 19.

- Referring to the photo, lay out the rows so the blocks continue to alternate. Stitch them together.
- Stitch a 1 1/2" x 80" white strip between a 1 1/2" x 80" navy print strip and a 1" x 80" red print strip, along their length, to form a pieced border. Make 4.
- Measure the length of the quilt. Trim 2 of the pieced borders to that measurement and stitch them to the long sides of the quilt, placing the navy print against the quilt.
- Measure the width of the quilt, including the borders. Trim the remaining pieced borders to that measurement and stitch them to the remaining sides of the quilt in the same manner.
- Finish the quilt as described in the *General Directions,* using the 2 1/2" x 44" red strips for the binding.

"Dove in the Window"

My husband purchased an antique quilt top at an auction in the Kansas countryside. I recognized that a quilter had carefully pieced the blocks in the 1800s but someone else later stitched the sashing in a slapdash manner with whatever fabrics were about the house. The quilt had shirting fabrics with a button or two still clinging, delicate silk fabrics about to fray, and striped dress and shirting fabrics in wild colors. The blocks simply cried out to be removed from the sashing with loving care, and the person to do it would be me.

As my pile of rust and blue Dove in the Window blocks grew, I knew I had a real treasure. But when I arranged them on my "quilt bed," I realized the blue blocks and the rust blocks were of two different sizes—one with a seam allowance and the other without. I set the blue blocks in the "Doves in the Window," wallhanging which I quilted in our van while my husband went trout fishing near Mountain Grove, Arkansas. When we returned home, I reset the rust blocks with brown fabric. Now I have two lovely, antique quilts. How glad I am that the blocks were not compatible sizes!

Dove in the Window

Use polka dots to set off vintage or vintage-style blocks to perfection.

QUILT SIZE: 59 1/2" square
BLOCK SIZE: 10" square

MATERIALS
- Assorted dark prints totaling at least 1 1/2 yards
- Assorted light prints totaling at least 3/4 yard
- 2 1/4 yards blue pindot
- 3/4 yard navy pindot
- 1 1/2 yards white print for the inner border
- 3 3/4 yards backing fabric
- 64" square of batting

CUTTING
The diamond pattern (on page 28) is full size and includes a 1/4" seam allowance. Make a template for the pattern piece. Trace around the template on the right side of the fabric and cut the pieces out on the drawn lines. Cut the lengthwise blue pin dot and white print strips before cutting smaller pieces from those fabrics.
NOTE: *In the original quilt, some of the blocks consist of 4 matching sections while others include some sections which are either slightly or wildly mismatched. In the interest of clarity, the directions provide for all matching sections. If you wish to use mismatched sections, refer to the quilt photo for guidance, and cut the diamonds from a wide variety of prints.*
For each of 9 blocks:
- Cut 8: diamonds, first dark print
- Cut 8: diamonds, second dark print
- Cut 2: 3 3/8" squares, third dark print, then cut them in half diagonally to yield 4 triangles
- Cut 1: 2" square, fourth dark print
- Cut 4: 2 1/4" squares, light print
- Cut 4: 2" x 4 3/4" strips, light print
- Cut 2: 3 3/4" squares, light print, then cut them in quarters diagonally to yield 8 triangles

Also:
- Cut 4: 1 3/4" x 49" lengthwise strips, white print, for the inner border
- Cut 4: 6 1/2" x 61" lengthwise strips,

blue pindot, for the outer border
- Cut 24: 4" x 10 1/2" strips, blue pindot
- Cut 6: 2 1/4" x 44" strips, navy pindot, for the binding
- Cut 16: 4" squares, navy pindot

DIRECTIONS
For each block:
- Stitch 2 first dark print diamonds together as shown. Make 4.
- Stitch a second dark print diamond to each first dark print diamond.

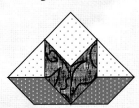

- Set a 2 1/4" light print square and 2 light print triangles into the diamond unit.

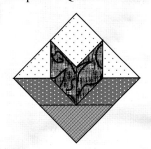

- Stitch a third dark print triangle to the unit to complete a Quarter-Block. Make 4.

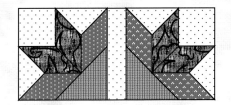

- Stitch a 2" x 4 3/4" light print strip between 2 Quarter-Blocks to make a Half-Block. Make 2.

- Stitch the 2" fourth dark print square between two 2" x 4 3/4" light print strips.
- Stitch this pieced strip between the Half-Blocks to complete a Dove in the Window block. Make 9.

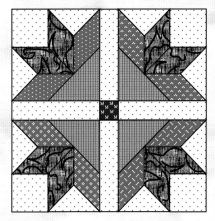

ASSEMBLY
- Lay out 3 blocks alternately with four 4" x 10 1/2" blue pindot strips. Stitch them into a row. Make 3.
- Stitch four 4" navy pindot squares and three 4" x 10 1/2" blue pindot strips together alternately to make a pieced sashing. Make 4.

- Lay out the rows alternately with pieced sashings. Stitch them together.
- Measure the quilt through the center. Trim 2 of the 1 3/4" x 49" white print strips to that measurement. Stitch them to opposite sides of the quilt.
- Measure the quilt, including the borders. Trim the remaining 1 3/4" x 49" white print strips to that measurement. Stitch them to the remaining sides of the quilt.
- In the same manner, trim 2 of the 6 1/2" x 61" blue pindot strips to fit the quilt's width and stitch them to opposite sides.
- Trim the remaining 6 1/2" x 61" blue pindot strips to fit the quilt's length and stitch them to the remaining sides.
- Finish the quilt as described in the *General Directions*, using the 2 1/2" x 44" navy pindot strips for the binding.

"Dresden Plate"

No wonder the Dresden Plate was such a favorite. Made with scraps, the plates can be set together and then appliquéd on white or colored fabric. Set together with sashing, it gets a completely new look. The Kansas City Star newspaper and many quilt books from the 1930s offered this pattern. Many quiltmakers during that period made at least one Dresden Plate.

This Thirties quilt top came from my favorite source of old quilt tops—Butler, Missouri. It's where I have found many of my finest examples in mint condition. Now that my secret is out, the town will not be the same. The Dresden Plate quilt top was made entirely by hand and put away by a woman who must have lived well into her eighties or nineties. Her relatives sold this top along with her laundered feedsacks at auction. The only other bidder was a quilt dealer, so I bought it without feeling I was cheating a family member out of an heirloom they wanted to keep.

When I got home, I started to quilt the top. With the cotton fabrics of the Thirties smooth under my fingers, the quilting went quickly. I saved the quilting of the sashing for last because I couldn't decide what pattern to use. I searched through all my magazines and books but found nothing that appealed to me. Then I remembered my calendar of antique quilts. That is where I found the quilting design for the yellow sashing.

Finding a matching yellow fabric for the binding proved to be a problem until I attended yet another auction in Butler. There I found the color that was just right. Today the quilt is bound and ready for a new life.

I've wondered why so many lovely quilt tops keep cropping up in an unfinished condition. Did quiltmakers simply love to piece quilts but hate the process of quilting? I have been told that women used to piece a quilt top as a wedding gift. They then got together after the bride was married and quilted it for her. I like to think they always wanted to be prepared to present the next bride with a lovely quilt top made entirely by hand.

Dresden Plate

A common design but always a favorite!

QUILT SIZE: 76" x 94"
BLOCK SIZE: 14" square

MATERIALS
- 4 1/4 yards muslin
- 2 1/2 yards bright yellow
- 3/4 yard light yellow
- Assorted print scraps totaling 3 1/2 yards
- 5 3/4 yards backing fabric
- 80" x 98" piece of batting

CUTTING
The wedge pattern (on page 28) includes a 1/4" seam allowance as do all dimensions given.
For each of 20 blocks:
- Cut 22: wedges, assorted prints
Also:
- Cut 20: 15" squares, muslin
- Cut 5: 4 1/2" x 86 1/2" strips, bright yellow
- Cut 2: 4 1/2" x 76 1/2" strips, bright yellow
- Cut 15: 4 1/2" x 14 1/2" strips, bright yellow
- Cut 9: 2 1/2" x 44" strips, light yellow, for the binding

DIRECTIONS
For each block:
- Place 2 print wedges right sides together. Stitch them together, stopping at the dots and backstitching, as shown. Make 11.

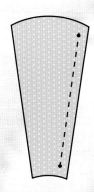

- Stitch the pairs together in the same manner to make a plate.
- Center the plate on a 15" muslin square and pin it in place.

- Appliqué the inner and outer edges of the plate to the square, turning under the seam allowances as you go. You may want to trim the turn-under allowances slightly for ease in turning and to reduce bulk. Make 20.

- Trim each block to 14 1/2" square.

ASSEMBLY
- Lay out 5 blocks alternately with four 4 1/2" x 14 1/2" bright yellow strips. Sew them together to make a row. Make 4.
- Lay out the 4 1/2" x 86 1/2" bright yellow strips alternately with the rows. Sew them together.
- Sew the 4 1/2" x 76 1/2" bright yellow strips to the short sides of the quilt.
- Finish the quilt as described in the *General Directions,* using the 2 1/2" x 44" light yellow strips for the binding.

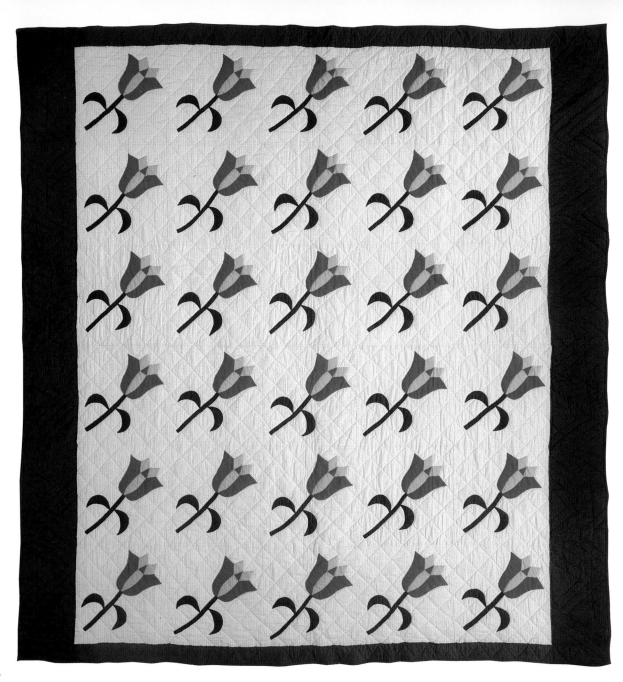

"Tulips"

Estate auctions are especially sad when a respected citizen of the community can no longer live alone after many years of dedicated service. Such was the case when the contents of Blind Johnny Smith's home in LaCygne, Kansas, were auctioned. Among his lifetime accumulation of possessions were several very old quilts, including this Tulip quilt top in the ancient red, deep yellow, and that shade of green which is peculiar to the 1860s. Apparently someone in Johnny's family or his wife's family, no one knew for sure, made the quilt top shortly after the Civil War ended. No one had dared to quilt it through the years. No mice had chewed at the corners. It had only one bug stain. In short, it was practically in mint condition.

An acquaintance who had admired the quilt also waited all day for the quilts to sell. When I began bidding, I kept my eyes on the auctioneer, but I knew who else was bidding on the quilt top. When the bidding ceased and the auctioneer called out "sold," it was mine for $65, more than I had ever paid for a quilt top up until then.

At home, I began basting the back, the batting, and the beautiful top together. What a joy it was to quilt the old, soft cottons which seemed to grow more mellow as the years went by! I loved outlining each tulip and didn't overquilt the top. When I finished binding "Tulips," I spread it on my big white bed with the brass knobs, but something was wrong. Completely dwarfed in my small room, it cried out for a large bedroom like one in those old Southern mansions. So I folded it and put it away, but every now and then I take the quilt out and admire the tulips tossing beautifully as though a soft wind has stirred them. It saddens me that Blind Johnny could never see this lovely, old quilt finished. I've often admired those tiny appliqué stitches, so close and so well done. I doubt the quilter's work would have survived the hard use through the winters of Iowa, Missouri, or Kansas had it been completed. Her antique quilt has become one of my most treasured possessions.

Tulips

Reproduce this antique quilt to welcome summer days.

QUILT SIZE: 89 1/2" x 92"
BLOCK SIZE: 14 1/2" square

MATERIALS

- 6 3/4 yards muslin
- 1 yard green
- 1 1/2 yards red
- 1/2 yard gold
- 2 3/4 yards green with white dots for the border and binding
- 7 3/4 yards backing fabric
- 94" x 96" piece of batting

CUTTING

The appliqué leaf and stem patterns (on page 29) are full size and do not include a turn-under allowance. Make a template for each of the pattern pieces. Trace around the templates on the right side of the fabrics and add a 1/8" to 3/16" turn-under allowance when cutting the fabric pieces out. Hand-piecing patterns A, B, C, and D are full size and do not include a seam allowance. Trace aound the templates on the wrong side of the fabric and add a 1/4" seam allowance when cutting the pieces out. All other dimensions include a 1/4" seam allowance.

- Cut 30: 15 1/2" squares, muslin
- Cut 30: stems, green
- Cut 60: leaves, green
- Cut 30: A, red
- Cut 30: B, gold
- Cut 60: C, gold
- Cut 30: D, red
- Cut 30: DR, red
- Cut 2: 9" x 88" strips, green with white dots, for the border
- Cut 2: 3" x 92" strips, green with white dots, for the border
- Cut 5: 2 1/2" x 88" strips, green with white dots, for the binding

DIRECTIONS

For each block:

- Lightly press a 15 1/2" muslin square

in half diagonally. Open the square and fold it in half again from top to bottom and from side to side and press.

- Using the pressed lines as a reference, pin a green stem slightly above the center, where the fold lines intersect, and gently curving away from the diagonal fold. Appliqué it in place. There is no need to turn under or stitch the end of the stem that will be overlapped by the tulip.
- Pin 2 green leaves in place, as shown, and appliqué.

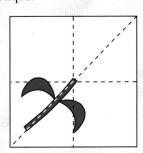

- Stitch a red A to a gold B. Stitch 2 gold C's to the unit. Stitch a red D and a red DR to the unit to make a tulip.

- Pin the tulip in place, covering the end

of the stem and centering it on the pressed diagonal line, as shown.

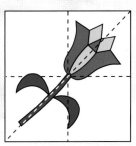

- Appliqué the tulip in place. Press the block from the wrong side.
- Trim the block to 15" square, keeping the appliqué centered. Make 30.

ASSEMBLY

- Lay out the blocks in 6 rows of 5.
- Stitch the blocks into rows. Join the rows.
- Measure the length of the quilt. Trim the 9" x 88" green with white dots strips to that measurement. Stitch them to the sides of the quilt.
- Measure the width of the quilt, including the borders. Trim the 3" x 92" green with white dots strips to that measurement and stitch them to the top and bottom of the quilt.
- Finish the quilt as described in the *General Directions*, using the 2 1/2" x 88" green with white dots strips for the binding.

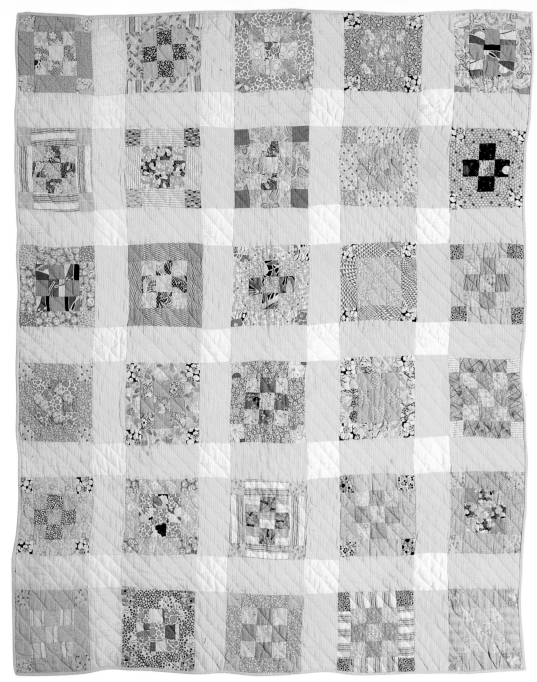

"Ariel's 'Blankie"

When our great-granddaughter Ariel was not yet two-years old, she was putting sentences together. When she stayed overnight with us, I laid out sheets and a quilt for her on the living room floor. She snuggled under this little Nine Patch and went to sleep right away. A couple of months later, she stayed over and I made her bed on the floor once again. I had forgotten to give Ariel the quilt as a blanket this time, but she remembered. "Where is my blankie?" she asked. Ariel then got up, went to the quilt rack, and pulled off the Nine Patch. "Here's my blankie," she declared. Hence the name "Ariel's 'Blankie'."

I almost didn't buy the Nine Patch quilt top at an auction in LaCygne, Kansas, not only because it was small and dirty, but because I felt its bright green and red border was harsh. It had been thrown haphazardly into a box with other unattractive fabrics. I actually had my eyes set on a wine and white Wedding March. It was that quilt that had attracted a great

deal of interest from quilters who kept spreading it out, admiring its design and the quality of its workmanship. No one looked twice at the Nine Patch with the ugly border.

I was the highest bidder for the Wedding March quilt. After that, the Nine Patch was held up for sale. Half-heartedly I purchased it for eight dollars. Before I could quilt it, however, I removed the bright green and red border, washed the quilt by hand, and then laid it on the patio to dry in the sun. When I began ironing it, I realized what a nice quilt it would be for one of my grandchildren to sleep under.

I used a soft polyester batting I had left over from another quilting project and a feedsack for the back. When I quilted it my needle simply flew through the fabrics. The little quilt turned out to be soft and cuddly.

It's surprising to realize the quilt I almost didn't buy has become one of my favorites. Once it was quilted, it took on a new life. I wonder who pieced the charming quilt back in the 1930s when I was a little girl myself.

Ariel's Blankie

Yellow sashings provide year-round sunshine.

QUILT SIZE: 56" x 68"
BLOCK SIZE: 8" square

MATERIALS
- Assorted vintage or reproduction 1930s prints, each at least 5" x 9", and totaling at least 1 1/2 yards
- 2 1/4 yards yellow
- 1/2 yard white
- 3 1/2 yards backing fabric
- 60" x 72" piece of batting

CUTTING
Dimensions include a 1/4" seam allowance.
For each of 30 blocks:
- Cut 5: 2" squares, first print
- Cut 4: 2" squares, second print
- Cut 4: 2 1/4" x 5" strips, third print
- Cut 4: 2 1/4" squares, fourth print

Also:
- Cut 20: 4 1/2" squares, white
- Cut 49: 4 1/2" x 8 1/2" strips, yellow
- Cut 7: 2 1/2" x 44" strips, yellow, for the binding

DIRECTIONS
For each block:
- Lay out the 2" squares, alternating the prints, as shown. Stitch the squares into rows and join the rows to complete a Nine Patch.

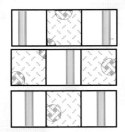

- Stitch 2 1/4" x 5" third print strips to 2 opposite sides of the Nine Patch.

- Stitch 2 1/4" fourth print squares to the ends of the 2 remaining third print strips. Stitch them to the remaining sides of the Nine Patch to complete a block. Make 30.

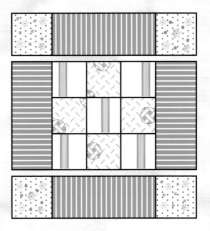

ASSEMBLY
- Referring to the quilt photo, lay out 5 blocks alternately with four 4 1/2" x 8 1/2" yellow strips. Stitch them together to form a row. Make 6.
- Lay out five 4 1/2" x 8 1/2" yellow strips alternately with four 4 1/2" white squares. Stitch them together to form a pieced sashing. Make 5.
- Lay out the rows alternately with the pieced sashings and stitch them together.
- Finish the quilt as described in the *General Directions*, using the 2 1/2" x 44" yellow strips for the binding.

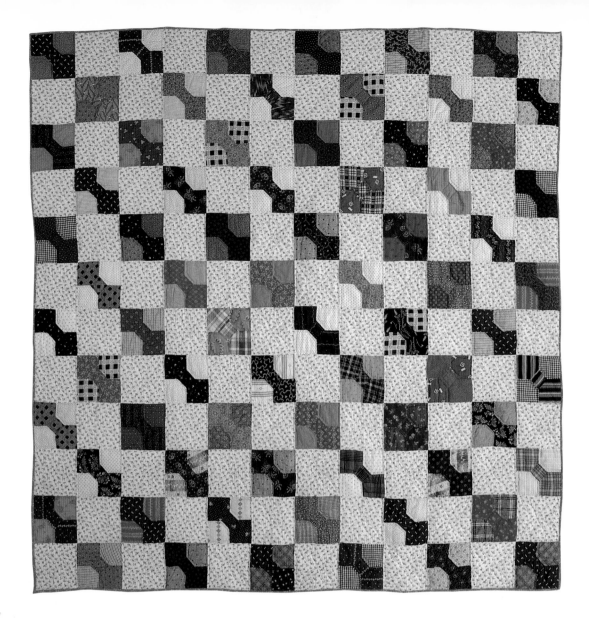

"Neckties"

"Neckties" was one of many quilts for sale at an auction southwest of Prescott, Kansas. I hadn't inspected the quilt tops well, for I had my heart set on Postage Stamp and Strippy blocks made of fabric from the 1880s. These works by the same quiltmaker made me think of the old saying:
"A maid who is quiltless at 21 shall never greet her bridal sun." Clearly this quiltmaker had not been quiltless at that age.

Standing in the rain at that auction, I watched a Flower Garden quilt top sell rather high considering its poor condition. Next up was a Double Wedding Ring. It, too, quickly soared out of my budget. Then a series of utility quilts sold and the prices began to drop. I bought the box with the strip pieced blocks for $20 and then the Postage Stamp blocks for $8. I thought I was finished for the day when the auctioneer held up the last quilt top. I recognized it at once as the Necktie pattern done in old 19th-century fabrics. The bidding stopped with my $7 bid. I went home that day at 3:30 p.m., soaking wet but very happy.

When I unpacked my treasures, I realized what a fine buy I had made with the Necktie quilt top. It had several conversation pieces, yet some of its materials didn't look as old as the neckties. The squares between the neckties were

prints of small roses with green leaves, not the sort of fabric one finds in the 19th century. I realized then what probably had happened. A quilter made enough neckties for a full-sized quilt and put them aside. Around the turn of the century, another quiltmaker picked up the blocks and set them together with the rose-printed material. She neglected to quilt her top for a reason I do not know.

Then I came along in 1995, the proud owner of this traditional quilt. I purchased batting and immediately began putting the quilt together. While my husband snoozed in his chair before the television, I put the first stitches in my "new" quilt. In three weeks' time the Necktie was finished. Another rescued quilt top ready for use. Among the three of us—the one who pieced the blocks, the one who set the blocks together, and myself—the quilt was finally complete.

I could not see "Neckties" machine quilted or remaining unquilted. Nor could I see it put away or sold at an antique shop. I could not imagine it any way but hand quilted. While quilting the neckties, I was elated to find unusual patterns such as anchors printed on some of the fabrics. I am certain this quilt, which I initially had not intended to buy, truly was meant for me.

Neckties

You don't need a formal occasion to show off these bow ties.

QUILT SIZE: 78" square
BLOCK SIZE: 6 1/2" square

MATERIALS

- Assorted dark prints totaling at least 2 1/2 yards
- Assorted light to medium prints totaling at least 2 yards
- 2 1/2 yards white print
- 3/4 yard pink print
- 7 yards backing fabric
- 82" square of batting

CUTTING

Patterns A and B (on page 27) are full size and include a 1/4" seam allowance as do all dimensions given. Make a template for each pattern piece.

For each of 72 blocks:

- Cut 2: A, one dark print
- Cut 1: B, same dark print; or cut a 2 1/2" square
- Cut 2: A, light or medium print

Also:

- Cut 72: 7" squares, white print
- Cut 8: 2 1/2" x 44" strips, pink print, for the binding

DIRECTIONS

For each block:

- Stitch a 2 1/2" dark print square to a matching dark print A between the dots, as shown, backstitching at each dot.

- Stitch a dark print A to the opposite side of the square in the same manner.
- Set matching light or medium print A's into the remaining sides of the unit to complete a block. Make 72.

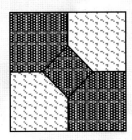

ASSEMBLY

- Lay out 6 blocks alternately with six 7" white print squares, keeping all of the bow ties tilted in the same direction. Stitch them together to complete a row. Make 12.
- Referring to the quilt photo, lay out the rows and stitch them together.
- Finish the quilt as described in the *General Directions,* using the 2 1/2" x 44" pink print strips for the binding

SPEED-PIECING VARIATION

Cutting is for the blocks only.

CUTTING

Dimensions include a 1/4" seam allowance.

For each of 72 blocks:

- Cut 2: 3 3/4" squares, dark print
- Cut 2: 2" squares, same dark print
- Cut 2: 3 3/4" squares, light print

DIRECTIONS

- Draw a diagonal line from corner to corner on the wrong side of each 2" dark print square.
- Lay a marked square on a 3 3/4" light or medium print square, right sides together, and stitch on the drawn line, as shown.

- Press the square toward the corner, aligning the edges. Trim the seam allowance to 1/4". Make 2.
- Stitch each unit to a matching 3 3/4" dark print square, as shown.

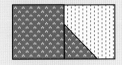

- Stitch them together to complete a block. Make 72.

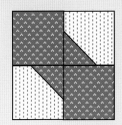

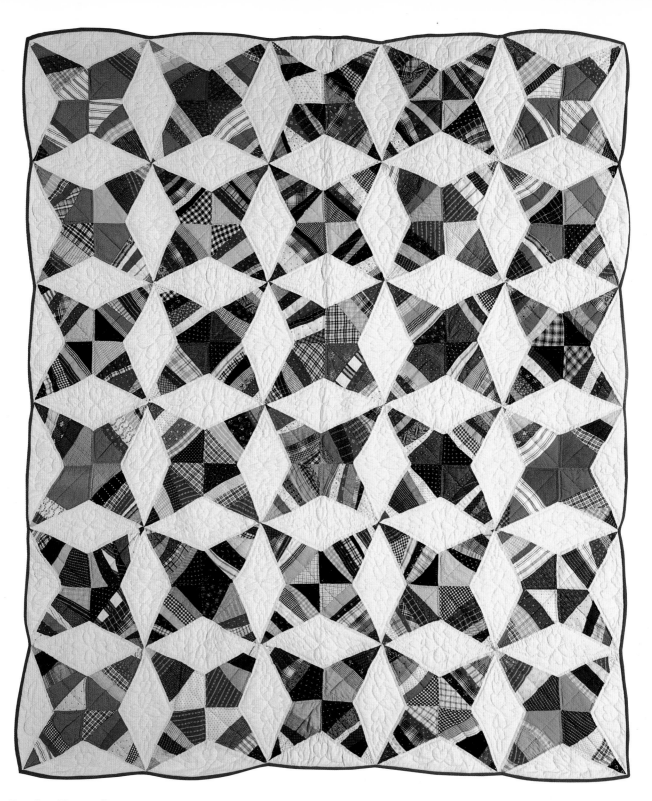

"Rocky Road to Kansas"

I purchased the beautiful, old strip-pieced blocks of "Rocky Road to Kansas" one rainy day at a sale near Prescot, Kansas. They had been pieced on wrapping paper from a Mound City, Kansas, general store which sold everything from needles to combines—a Walmart of the 1800s. I had no idea what pattern they were, but I knew they were very, very old and that I had to have them, paper and all. So I stood in the pouring rain and waited.

The quilt blocks went for $20. I paid this and felt they were worth every penny. Still not knowing the name of the pattern,

I took them home and put them away. Then I received a copy of a book showing historic Kansas quilts. There it was—my Rocky Road to Kansas!

I knew I would set it together with muslin, but summer was fast approaching and the yard demanded my attention. I returned to the Rocky Road quilt in the fall and found its diamond sections challenged me. I had to sit down and set each section in by hand so the whole thing wouldn't stretch and pucker. Finally, the top was ready to quilt.

Today, the strip-pieced Rocky Road quilt is one of my favorite treasures.

Rocky Road to Kansas

Here's the perfect quilt for using up a wide variety of scraps!

QUILT SIZE: 60" x 72"
BLOCK SIZE: 12" square

MATERIALS
- Assorted scraps ranging from dark to light and totaling at least 4 yards
- 3 yards muslin
- 5/8 yard red for the binding
- 4 yards backing fabric
- 64" x 76" piece of batting
- Paper for the foundations

CUTTING
Foundation pattern A (on page 30) is full size and does not include a seam allowance. Pattern B is full size and includes a 1/4" seam allowance as do all dimensions given.
- Cut 71: B, muslin
- Cut 7: 2 1/2" x 44" strips, red, for the binding

DIRECTIONS
- Trace the full-size A pattern, including the placement line, 120 times on the foundation paper. Cut the foundations out on the outer lines.
- Begin by positioning a fabric scrap right side up on the wide end of the foundation, placing the edge on or near the drawn line, as shown. Be sure the scrap extends at least 1/4" beyond all sides of the section it will cover.

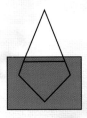

- Hold the scrap in place with a pin or a dab of glue from a glue stick, if desired.
- Lay the straight edge of another scrap right side down on the first one, aligning the edge, as shown. Stitch 1/4" from the raw edges through both scraps and the foundation.

NOTE: *The scraps in the quilt are not all parallel. Place some strips on an angle if desired.* Be sure that the edge of the underneath scrap is visible when placing the next scrap on top to ensure a 1/4" seam allowance. Make sure all scraps extend at least 1/4" beyond the edges of the foundation. Trim all seam allowances to 1/4" after stitching.

- Open the second scrap and press.
- Place a third scrap right side down on the second scrap. Stitch and trim, as before.
- Continue adding strips to the foundation in the same manner until the entire foundation is covered. To avoid bulk in the seams when the units are joined, do not use small pieces in the narrow end of the foundation.
- Trim the fabrics 1/4" beyond the edges of the foundation. Make 60 with a dark print on the wide end and 60 with a light print on the wide end. Pair 2 dark units with 2 light units when making the blocks.
- Stitch a dark foundation to a light foundation, as shown, backstitching at the dot. Make 2.

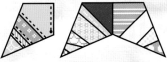

- Stitch them together to make a Star Unit. Make 30.

ASSEMBLY
- Lay out 5 Star Units in a row with white B's between them and at each end.

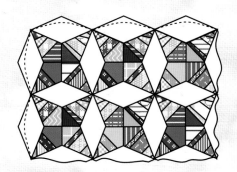

- Set in the B's between the Star Units to complete the row. Make 5.
- In the same manner, stitch the rows together with white B's between the Star Units.
- Trim the edges of the quilt 1/4" beyond the points of the outermost stars, trimming the outer B's in a slight curve. Refer to the quilt photo, as necessary.

- Carefully remove the paper foundations.
- Finish the quilt as described in the *General Directions*, using the 2 1/2" x 44" red strips for the binding.

Ocean Waves

(continued from page 9)

• In the same manner, stitch a dark Unit C to the right side of a large pink print triangle and a light Unit C to the left side of the large pink print triangle, as shown. Make 9.

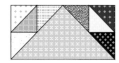

• Stitch a dark Unit C to a small pink print triangle, and a light Unit C to the remaining small pink print triangle to form 2 quarter-blocks.

• Referring to the Assembly Diagram lay out the blocks, half-blocks, quarter-blocks, and remaining Unit A's, rotating them as needed so that the light triangles in one block line up with the dark triangles in the adjoining blocks.

• Stitch the blocks into rows and join the rows.

• Finish the quilt as described in the *General Directions*, using the 2 1/2" x 44" light plaid strips for the binding.

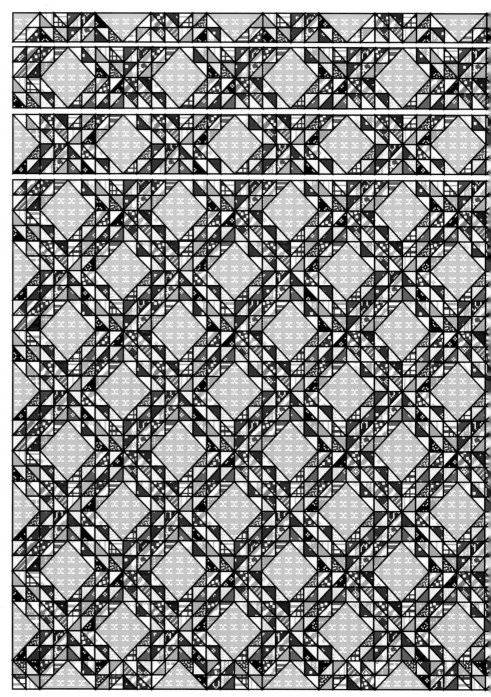

Patterns for
True Lover's Knot
(*Instructions begin
on page 5.*)

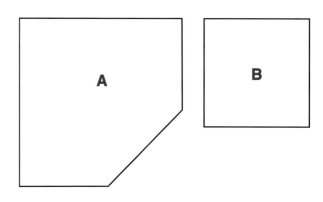

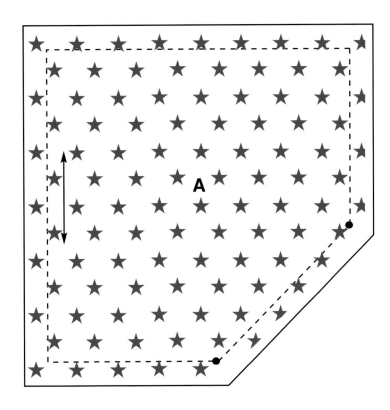

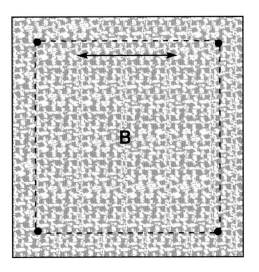

Full-size patterns for Neckties
(*Instructions are on page 23.*)

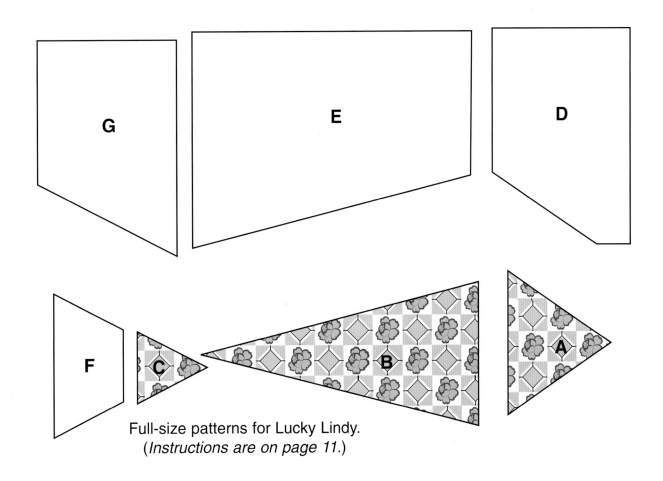

Full-size patterns for Lucky Lindy.
(*Instructions are on page 11.*)

Full-size wedge pattern for Dresden Plate.
(*Instructions are on page 17.*)

Full-size diamond pattern
for Dove in the Window
(*Instructions are on page 15.*)

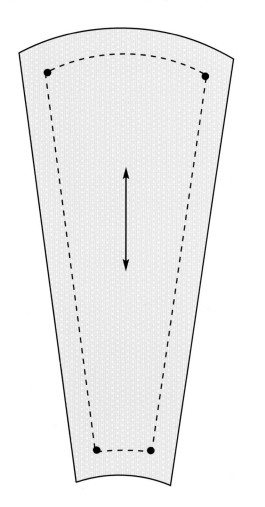

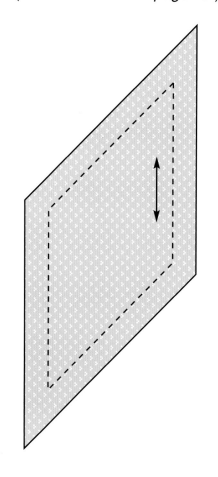

Full-size patterns for Missouri Daisy.
(*Instructions are on page 7.*)

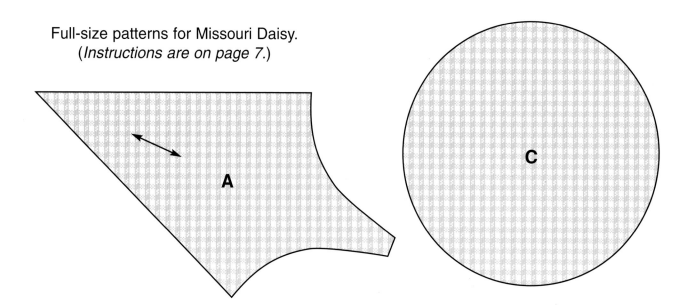

A

C

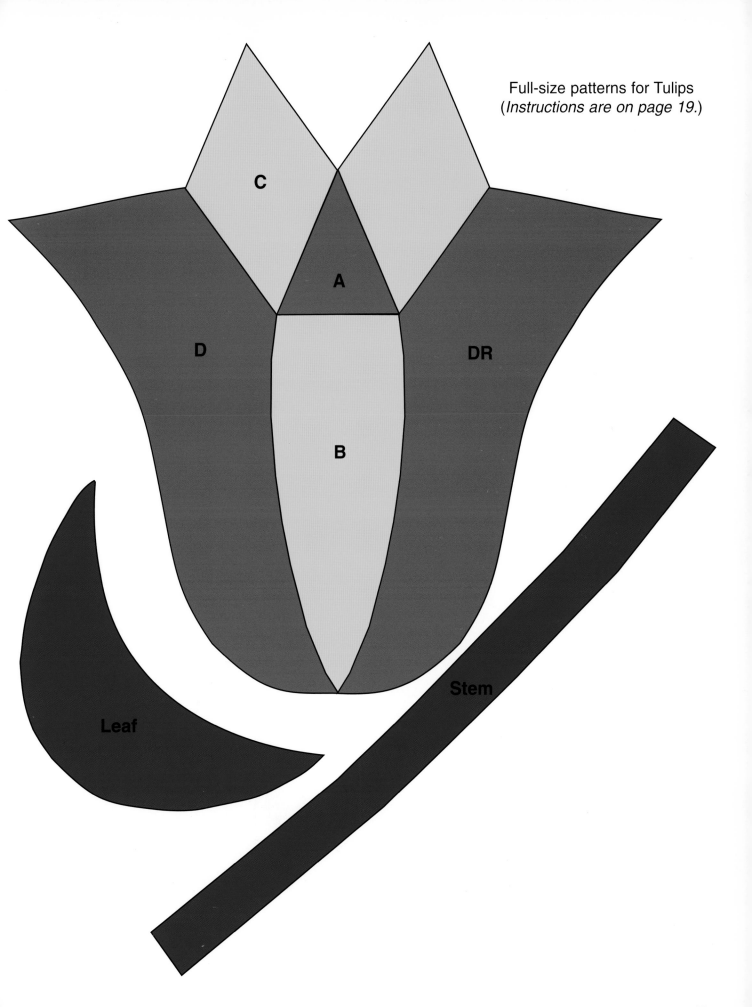

Full-size patterns for Tulips
(*Instructions are on page 19.*)

C

A

D

DR

B

Leaf

Stem

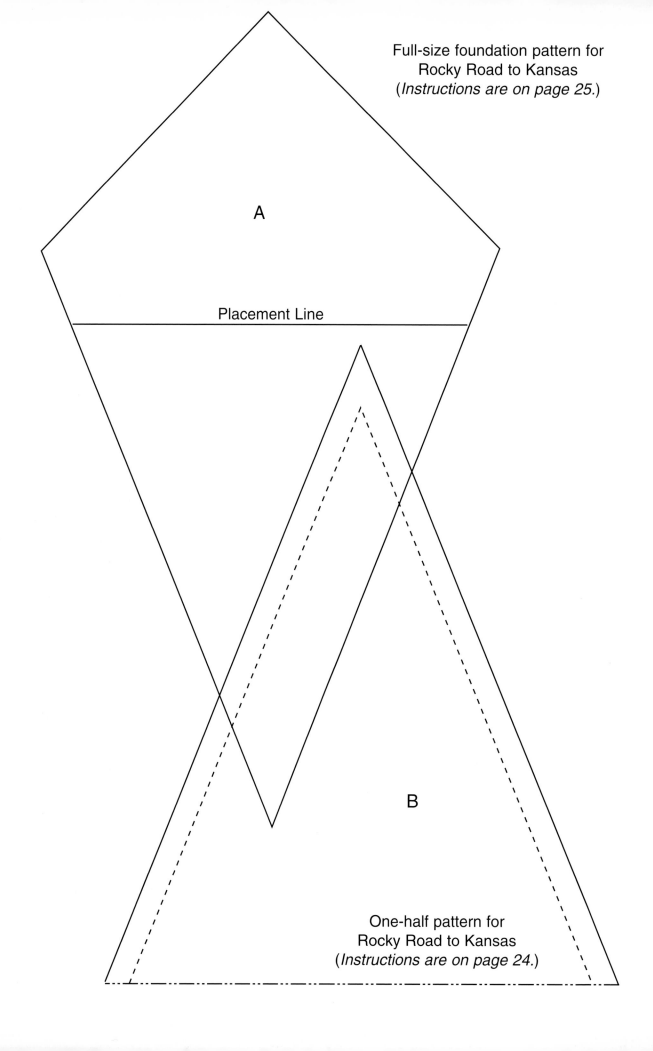

Full-size foundation pattern for
Rocky Road to Kansas
(*Instructions are on page 25.*)

A

Placement Line

B

One-half pattern for
Rocky Road to Kansas
(*Instructions are on page 24.*)

General Directions

ABOUT THE PATTERNS

Read through the pattern directions before cutting fabric. Yardage requirements are based on 44"-wide fabric with a useable width of 42". Pattern directions are given in step-by-step order. If you are sending your quilt to a professional machine quilter, consult them regarding the necessary batting and backing size for your quilt. Batting and backing dimensions listed in the patterns are for hand quilting.

FABRICS

We suggest using 100% cotton. Wash fabric in warm water with mild detergent and no fabric softener. Dry fabric on a warm-to-hot setting. Press with a hot dry iron to remove any wrinkles.

ROTARY CUTTING

Begin by folding the fabric in half, selvage to selvage. Make sure the selvages are even and the folded edge is smooth. Fold the fabric in half again, bringing the fold and the selvages together, again making sure everything is smooth and flat.

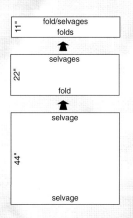

Position the folded fabric on a cutting mat so that the fabric extends to the left for right-handed people, or to the right for left-handed people.

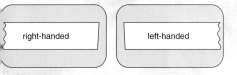

right-handed   left-handed

With the ruler resting on the fabric, line up the folded edge of the fabric with a horizontal line on the ruler. Trim the uneven edge with a rotary cutter. Make a clean cut through the fabric, beginning in front of the folds and cutting through to the opposite edge with one clean stroke. Always cut away from yourself never toward yourself!

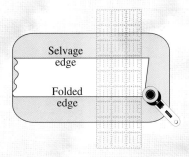

Selvage edge

Folded edge

Turn the mat 180°. Move the ruler to the proper width for cutting the first strip and continue cutting until you have the required number of strips. To keep the cut edges even, always move the ruler, not the fabric. Open up one fabric strip and check the spots where there were folds. If the fabric was not evenly lined up or the ruler was incorrectly positioned, there will be a bend at each of the folds in the fabric.

When cutting many strips, check after every three or four strips to make sure the strips are straight.

TEMPLATES

Template patterns are full size and, unless otherwise noted, include a 1/4" seam allowance. The solid line is the cutting line; the dashed line is the stitching line. Place a sheet of firm, clear plastic over the patterns and trace the cutting line and/or stitching line for each one. Templates for machine piecing include a seam allowance, templates for hand piecing generally do not.

MARKING THE FABRIC

Test marking tools for removability before using them. Sharpen pencils often. Align the grainline on the template with the grainline of the fabric. Place a piece of fine sandpaper beneath the fabric to prevent slipping, if desired. For machine piecing, mark the right side of the fabric. For hand piecing, mark the wrong side of the fabric, and flip asymmetrical templates before tracing them. Mark and cut just enough pieces to make a sample block, piece it to be sure your templates are accurate.

PIECING

For machine piecing, sew 12 stitches per inch, exactly 1/4" from the edge of the fabric. To make accurate piecing easier, mark the throat plate with a piece of tape 1/4" away from the point where the needle pierces the fabric. Start and stop stitching at the cut edges except for set-in pieces. For set-ins, start and stop at the 1/4" seamlines and backstitch.

For hand piecing, begin with a small knot. Make one small backstitch and continue with a small running stitch, backstitching every 3-4 stitches. Stitch directly on the marked line from point to point, not edge to edge. Finish with 2 or 3 small backstitches before cutting the thread.

APPLIQUÉ

Mark the position of the pieces on the background. If the fabric is light, lay it over the pattern, matching centers and other indicators. Trace lightly. If the fabric is dark, use a light box or other light source to make tracing easier. To hand appliqué, baste or pin appliqué pieces to the background block in stitching order. Use a blindstitch or buttonhole stitch to appliqué the pieces. Do not turn under or stitch any edges that will be overlapped by other pieces.

Baste pieces (which have been cut on the traced line) in place with a long machine basting stitch or a narrow, open zigzag stitch. Then stitch over the basting with a short, wide satin stitch. Placing a piece of paper between the wrong side of the fabric and the feed dogs of the sewing machine will help stabilize the fabric. Carefully remove excess

(continued from page 31)

General Directions

paper when stitching is complete. You can also turn the edges of appliqué pieces under as for needleturn appliqué, and stitch them in place with a blind-hem stitch.

PRESSING

Press with a dry iron. Press seam allowances toward the darker of the two pieces whenever possible. Otherwise, trim away 1/16" from the darker seam allowance to prevent it from showing through. Press all blocks, sashings, and borders before assembling the quilt top.

FINISHING YOUR QUILT

Mark before basting the quilt top together with the batting and backing. Chalk pencils show well on dark fabrics, otherwise use a very hard (#3 or #4) pencil or other marker for this purpose. Test your marker first.

Transfer paper designs by placing fabric over the design and tracing. A light box may be necessary for darker fabrics. Precut plastic stencils that fit the area you wish to quilt may be placed on top of the quilt and traced. Use a ruler to mark straight, even grids. Masking tape can also be used to mark straight lines. Temporary quilting stencils can be made from clear adhesive-backed paper or freezer paper and reused many times. To avoid residue, do not leave tape or adhesive-backed paper on your quilt overnight.

Outline quilting does not require marking. Simply eyeball 1/4" from the seam or stitch "in the ditch" next to the seam. To prevent uneven stitching, try to avoid quilting through seam allowances wherever possible.

BASTING

Cut the batting and backing at least 4" larger than the quilt top. Tape the backing, wrong side up, on a flat surface to anchor it. Smooth the batting on top, followed by the quilt top, right side up. Baste the three layers together to form a quilt sandwich. Begin at the center and baste horizontally, then vertically. Add more lines of basting approximately every 6" until the entire top is secured.

QUILTING

Quilting is done with a short, strong needle

called a "between." The lower the number (size) of the needle, the larger it is. Begin with an 8 or 9 and progress to a 10 to 12. Use a thimble on the middle finger of the hand that pushes the needle. Begin quilting at the center of the quilt and work outward to keep the tension even and the quilting smooth.

Using an 18" length of quilting thread knotted at one end, insert the needle through the quilt top only and bring it up exactly where you will begin. Pop the knot through the fabric to bury it. Push the needle straight down into the quilt with 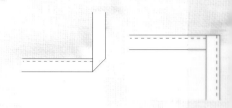 the thimbled finger of the upper hand and slightly depress the fabric in front of the needle with the thumb. Redirect the needle back to the top of the quilt using the middle or index finger of the lower hand.

Repeat with each stitch, using a rocking motion. Finish by knotting the thread close to the surface and popping the knot through the fabric to bury it. Remove basting when the quilting is complete.

If you wish to machine quilt, we recommend consulting one of the many fine books available on that subject.

BINDING

Cut binding strips with the grain for straight-edge quilts. To make 1/2" finished binding, cut 2 1/2"-wide strips. Sew the strips together with diagonal seams; trim and press the seam allowances open.

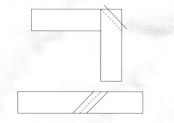

Fold the strip in half lengthwise, wrong side in, and press. Position the strip on the right side of the quilt top, aligning the raw edges of the binding with the edge of the quilt top. Leaving 6" of the binding strip free and beginning a few inches from one corner, stitch the binding to

the quilt with a 1/4" seam allowance. When you reach a corner, stop stitching 1/4" from the edge of the quilt top and backstitch. Clip the threads and remove the quilt from the machine. Fold the binding up and away from the quilt forming a 45° angle, as shown. Keeping the angled fold secure, fold the binding back down. This fold should be even with the edge of the quilt top. Begin stitching at the fold.

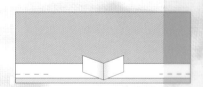

Continue stitching around the quilt in this manner to within 6" of the starting point. To finish, fold both strips back along the edge of the quilt so that the folded edges meet about 3" from both lines of stitching and the binding lies flat on the quilt. Finger press to crease the folds. Measure the width of the folded binding. Cut the strips that distance beyond the folds. (In this case 1 1/4" beyond the folds.)

Open both strips and place the ends at right angles to each other, right sides together. Fold the bulk of the quilt out of your way. Join the strips with a diagonal seam as shown.

Trim the seam allowance to 1/4" and press it open. Refold the strip wrong side in. Place the binding flat against the quilt, and finish stitching it to the quilt. Trim excess batting and backing so that the binding edge will be filled with batting when you fold the binding to the back of the quilt. Blindstitch the binding to the back, covering the seamline.

Remove visible markings. Sign and date your quilt.